The Book of ESTHER

for such a time as this...

Lederer Books

A division of

Messianic Jewish Publishers

Clarksville, MD 21029

Taken from the *Complete Jewish Bible*,
copyright © 1998, 2016 by David H. Stern.
Bible Story Summaries © 2018 by Barry and Lisa Rubin

Printed in the United States of America

Illustrations by Sweet Publishing
http://pub.distantshores.org/resources/illustrations/sweet-publishing

Graphic Design by Yvonne Vermillion,
Magic Graphix, West Fork, Arkansas

2018   1

ISBN 978-1-936716-95-1

Published by:
Lederer Books
A Division of Messianic Jewish Publishers & Resources
6120 Day Long Lane
Clarksville, MD 21029

Distributed by:
Messianic Jewish Publishers & Resources
Order line: (800) 410-7367
lederer@messianicjewish.net
www.MessianicJewish.net

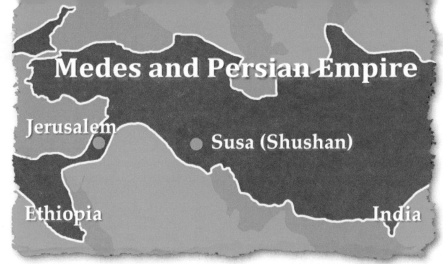

ESTHER
(ESTER)

Bavel (Babylon) was the Gentile world power that led Isra'el into captivity in three successive stages in 605, 597, and 587 B.C.E. In 539 B.C.E., Persia conquered Bavel, after which Koresh (Cyrus) issued the decree allowing the Jews to return to their homeland. Not all the Jews who had been taken captive elected to return, and many remained spread throughout the Persian Empire. The book of Esther records events that centered in Shushan (Susa), one of the four capitals of Persia, but affected all of the Jews residing in the Persian Empire, including those in Isra'el. Persian policy toward the Jews wavered. Koresh had allowed them to return to Isra'el, but Daryavesh (Darius) had put a halt to the rebuilding of the Temple until 520 B.C.E. At that time, Daryavesh rescinded this policy and allowed them to continue. After the completion of the Temple, some Jewish enemies wrote an accusation against the Jews. The book of Esther records that Achashverosh (Ahasuerus or Xerxes) allowed a decree to be written a few years later (ca. 474 B.C.E.) to destroy all Jews (3:7). However, on the basis of Queen Ester's intercession, he allows the Jews to defend themselves (chs. 8–9).

Notably, the book of Esther does not directly describe God's activity of controlling, overruling, or guiding the events of the story, nor is God's name mentioned. The fact that so many Jews did not return to Isra'el points to their reluctance in identifying with the God of Isra'el. Perhaps the geographical displacement and the spiritual indifference of the Jews helps explain the absence of such terms as "Temple," "sacrifice," "*Torah*," "prayer," and even "God." Nevertheless, the reader increasingly senses God's activity through the author's use of irony and through the placing and reversal of events. The absence of God's name does not indicate lack of involvement. God is actually very involved and near. Those who thought they were far from God find themselves under his scrutiny and care and are forced into action, which proves that God remains faithful and in sovereign control, even when the objects of his affection are unfaithful.

1

¹ These events took place in the time of Achashverosh, the Achashverosh who ruled over 127 provinces from India to Ethiopia. ² It was in those days, when King Achashverosh sat on his royal throne in Shushan the capital, ³ in the third year of his reign, that he gave a banquet for all his officials and courtiers. The army of Persia and Media, the nobles and the provincial officials were in attendance. ⁴ He displayed the dazzling wealth of his kingdom and his great splendor for a long time, 180 days. ⁵ At the end of that time, the king gave a seven-day banquet in the courtyard of the royal palace garden for all the people, both great and small, there in Shushan the capital. ⁶ There were white cotton curtains and blue hangings fastened to silver rods, with cords of fine linen and purple; the columns were marble; the couches [for reclining at table] were of gold and silver on a mosaic flooring of malachite, marble, mother-of-pearl and onyx. ⁷ Drinks were served in gold goblets, with each goblet different from the others. There was royal wine in abundance, as befits royal bounty. ⁸ The drinking was not according to any fixed rule, for the king had ordered the stewards to serve each man what he wanted. ⁹ Also Vashti the queen gave a banquet for the women in the royal house belonging to King Achashverosh.

¹⁰ On the seventh day, when the king was in high spirits from the wine, he ordered Mehuman, Bizta, Harvona, Bigta, Avagta, Zetar and Karkas, the seven officers who attended him, ¹¹ to bring Queen Vashti before the king with the royal crown, in order to show the people and the officials her beauty, for she was indeed a good-looking woman. ¹² But Queen Vashti refused to come at the order of the king, which he had sent through his officers. This enraged the king — his anger blazed inside him.

King Achashverosh was the most powerful man in the world, ruling over the empire of the Medes and Persians which stretched over 127 provinces from Ethiopia to India. In the third year of his reign he invited the nobles and princes to two feasts, one lasting 180 days, the other 7. Everyone drank from cups of gold.

Queen Vashti also gave a party for the women in another part of the palace. At the end of the feast the king, who was drunk, ordered Queen Vashti to show off her beauty. But the queen refused to join him. The king was furious.

¹³ As was the king's custom, he consulted sages well-versed in matters of law and justice. ¹⁴ With him were Karshna, Shetar, Admata, Tarshish, Meres, Marsna and Memukhan, the seven vice-regents of Persia and Media, who were part of the king's inner circle and were the most important officials in the kingdom. ¹⁵ [The king asked the sages,] "According to the law, what should we do to Queen Vashti, since she didn't obey the order of King Achashverosh conveyed by the officers?"

¹⁶ Memukhan presented the king and vice-regents this answer: "Vashti the queen has wronged not only the king, but also all the officials and all the peoples in all the provinces of King Achashverosh; ¹⁷ because this act of the queen's will become known to all the women, who will then start showing disrespect toward their own husbands; they will say, 'King Achashverosh ordered Vashti the queen to be brought before him, but she wouldn't come.' ¹⁸ Moreover, the noble ladies of Persia and Media who hear of the queen's conduct will mention it to all the king's officials, which will bring about no end of disrespect and discord. ¹⁹ If it pleases his majesty, let him issue a royal decree — and let it be written as one of the laws of the Persians and Medes, which are irrevocable — that Vashti is never again to be admitted into the presence of King Achashverosh, and that the king give her royal position to someone better than she. ²⁰ When the edict made by the king is proclaimed throughout the length and breadth of the kingdom, then all wives will honor their husbands, whether great or small."

²¹ This advice pleased the king and the officials, so the king did what Memukhan had suggested — ²² he sent letters to all the royal provinces, to each province in its own script and to each people in their own language, that every man should be master in his own house and speak the language of his own people.

The king's wise men advised him saying, *The queen has not only insulted you but everyone. She has set a bad example in not showing honor to her husband.* The Queen's title was taken away from her. A permanent law was made and read throughout the land that all wives must honor and obey their husbands.

2 ¹ A while later, when King Achashverosh's anger had subsided, he remembered Vashti, what she had done and what had been decreed against her. ² The king's servants attending him said, "A search should be made for young, good-looking virgins. ³ The king should appoint officials in all the provinces of the kingdom to gather all the young, good-looking virgins to the house for the harem, in Shushan the capital. They should be put under the care of Hegai the king's officer in charge of the women, and he should give them the cosmetics they require. ⁴ Then, the girl who seems best to the king should become queen instead of Vashti." This proposal pleased the king, so he acted accordingly.

⁵ There was in Shushan the capital a man who was a Jew, whose name was Mordekhai the son of Ya'ir, the son of Shim'i, the son of Kish, a Binyamini. ⁶ He had been exiled from Yerushalayim with the captives exiled with Y'khanyah king of Y'hudah, whom N'vukhadnetzar king of Bavel had carried off. ⁷ He had raised Hadassah, that is, Ester, his uncle's daughter; because she had neither father nor mother. The girl was shapely and good-looking; after her father's and mother's death, Mordekhai had adopted her as his own daughter.

⁸ When the king's order and decree were proclaimed, and many girls assembled in Shushan the capital under the care of Hegai, Ester too was taken into the king's house and put under the care of Hegai, who was in charge of the women. ⁹ The girl pleased him and won his favor, so that he lost no time in giving her her cosmetics, her portions [of special food] and seven girls from the king's palace to attend her; he also promoted her and the girls attending her to the best place in the harem's quarters. ¹⁰ Ester did not disclose her people or family ties, because Mordekhai had instructed her not to tell anyone. ¹¹ Every day Mordekhai would walk around in front of the courtyard of the harem's house in order to know how Ester was doing and what was happening to her.

¹² Each girl had her turn to appear before King Achashverosh after she had undergone the full twelve-month preparation period prescribed for the women, consisting of a six-month treatment with oil of myrrh and six months with perfumes and other cosmetics for women. ¹³ Then, when the girl went to see the king, whatever she wanted would be given to her as she went from the harem's house to the king's palace. ¹⁴ She would go in the evening, and on the following day she would return to another part of the harem's house and be under the care of Sha'ashgaz the king's officer in charge of the concubines. She would not go to the king again unless he was especially pleased with her and had her summoned by name.

¹⁵ When the turn came for Ester the daughter of Avichayil, whom Mordekhai had adopted as his own daughter, to appear before the king, she didn't ask for anything other than what Hegai the king's officer in charge of the harem advised. Yet Ester was admired by all who saw her. ¹⁶ She was brought to King Achashverosh in his royal palace in the tenth month, Tevet, during the seventh year of his reign. ¹⁷ The king liked Ester more than any of his wives; none of the other virgins obtained such favor and approval from him. So he put the royal crown on her head and made her queen in place of Vashti.

¹⁸ The king then gave a great banquet in Ester's honor for all his officers and servants, decreed a holiday for the provinces and distributed gifts worthy of royal bounty.

Now the king wondered who would replace Vashti as queen? A search took place throughout the land for the most beautiful young woman. Many women were entered into the beauty contest and were brought to the palace under the supervision of Hegai, the king's servant.

Working in the palace was a Jew named Mordekhai. He had a cousin named Ester (also known as Hadassah), whom he had adopted after her parents had died. Ester was a beautiful young girl who was with the other contestants at the palace for 12 months of beauty treatments before the royal wedding. Mordekhai told her not to tell anyone she was a Jew. Of the many women chosen for the contest, Ester was the one the king loved most so she was crowned as queen instead of Vashti.

A feast was given in her honor. But she told no one she was a Jew.

¹⁹ When the girls would gather on other occasions, Mordekhai would sit at the King's Gate. ²⁰ Ester had not yet revealed her family ties or her people, as Mordekhai had ordered her; for Ester continued obeying what Mordekhai told her to do, as she had when he was raising her. ²¹ On one of those occasions, when Mordekhai was sitting at the King's Gate, two of the king's officers, Bigtan and Teresh, from the group in charge of the private entryways, became angry and conspired to assassinate King Achashverosh. ²² But Mordekhai learned about it and told Ester the queen. Ester reported it to the king, crediting Mordekhai. ²³ The matter was investigated, found to be true, and both were hanged on a stake. All this was recorded in the daily journal that was kept with the king.

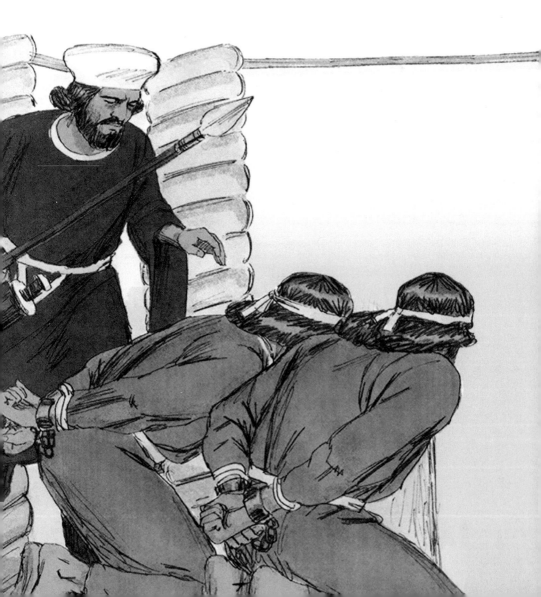

A little while later, when Mordekhai was guarding the king's gate, he overhead two servants, Bigtan and Teresh plotting against the king. Mordekhai immediately warned Ester of the plot, who told the king. The two plotters were arrested, found guilty and hung. Their plot was recorded in the chronicles of the king's reign where it was noted that Mordekhai had uncovered the plot.

3 ¹ Some time later King Achashverosh began to single out Haman the son of Hamdata the Agagi for advancement; eventually he gave him precedence over all his fellow officers. ² All the king's servants at the King's Gate would kneel and bow down before Haman, because the king had so ordered. But Mordekhai would neither kneel nor bow down to him. ³ The king's servants at the King's Gate asked Mordekhai, "Why don't you obey the king's order?" ⁴ But after they had confronted him a number of times without his paying attention to them, they told Haman, in order to find out whether Mordekhai's explanation that he was a Jew would suffice to justify his behavior. ⁵ Haman was furious when he saw that Mordekhai was not kneeling and bowing down to him. ⁶ However, on learning what people Mordekhai belonged to, it seemed to him a waste to lay hands on Mordekhai alone. Rather, he decided to destroy all of Mordekhai's people, the Jews, throughout the whole of Achashverosh's kingdom.

⁷ In the first month, the month of Nisan, in the twelfth year of Achashverosh, they began throwing *pur* (that is, they cast lots) before Haman every day and every month until the twelfth month, which is the month of Adar. ⁸ Then Haman said to Achashverosh, "There is a particular people scattered and dispersed among the peoples in all the provinces of your kingdom. Their laws are different from those of every other people; moreover, they don't observe the king's laws. It doesn't befit the king to tolerate them. ⁹ If it please the king, have a decree written for their destruction; and I will hand over 330 tons of silver to the officials in charge of the king's affairs to deposit in the royal treasury."

¹⁰ The king took his signet ring from his hand and gave it to Haman the son of Hamdata the Agagi, the enemy of the Jews. ¹¹ The king said to Haman, "The money is given to you, and the people too, to do with as seems good to you."

¹² The king's secretaries were summoned on the thirteenth day of the first month. They wrote down all Haman's orders to the king's army commanders and governors in all the provinces and to the officials of every people, to each province in its own script and to each people in their own language; everything was written in the name of King Achashverosh and sealed with the king's signet ring. ¹³ Letters were sent by courier to all the royal provinces "to destroy, kill and exterminate all Jews, from young to old, including small children and women, on a specific day, the thirteenth day of the twelfth month, the month of Adar, and to seize their goods as plunder." ¹⁴ A copy of the document to be issued as a decree in every province was to be publicly proclaimed to all the peoples, so that they would be ready for that day.

¹⁵ At the king's order the runners went out quickly, and the decree was issued in Shushan the capital. Then the king and Haman sat down for a drink together, but the city of Shushan was thrown into confusion.

Haman was an advisor to the king, who promoted him above all the other princes to become the second most powerful man in the kingdom. All the servants would bow to Haman when he entered, *except for Mordekhai,* because he was a Jew. This made Haman furious so he schemed to find a way to punish Mordekhai along with his people, the Jews. He convinced the king that the Jews were trouble: *A law must be passed so they can be destroyed. I will give 330 tons of silver to the king's treasury to get this done*, said Haman.

The king took off his signet ring and gave it to Haman. *Keep the money and do to these people what you think is best.* The king's scribes were instructed to write a law that on the 13th day of the 12th month (Adar) the Jews were to be attacked and killed and their possessions taken as plunder. This law could not be changed or altered and it was announced throughout the empire.

4 ¹ When Mordekhai learned everything that had been done, he tore his clothes, put on sackcloth and ashes and went out through the city, lamenting and crying bitterly. ² He stopped before entering the King's Gate, since no one was allowed to go inside the King's Gate wearing sackcloth. ³ In every province reached by the king's order and decree, there was great mourning among the Jews, with fasting, weeping and wailing, as many lay down on sackcloth and ashes.

⁴ When the girls and officials attending Ester came and informed her of this, the queen became deeply distressed. She sent clothes for Mordekhai to wear instead of his sackcloth, but he wouldn't accept them. ⁵ So Ester summoned Hatakh, one of the king's officials attending her, and instructed him to go to Mordekhai and find out what this was all about and why. ⁶ Hatakh went out to Mordekhai in the open space in front of the King's Gate, ⁷ and Mordekhai told him everything that had happened to him and exactly how much silver Haman had promised to put in the royal treasury for the destruction of the Jews. ⁸ He also gave him a copy of the decree for their destruction issued in Shushan; so that he could show it to Ester, explain it to her, and then instruct her to approach the king, intercede with him and implore his favor on behalf of her people. ⁹ Hatakh returned and told Ester what Mordekhai had said.

¹⁰ Then Ester spoke to Hatakh and gave him this message for Mordekhai: ¹¹ "All the king's officials, as well as the people in the royal provinces, know that if anyone, man or woman, approaches the king in the inner courtyard without being summoned, there is just one law — he must be put to death — unless the king holds out the gold scepter for him to remain alive; and I haven't been summoned to the king for the past thirty days."

¹² Upon being told what Ester had said, Mordekhai ¹³ asked them to give Ester this answer: "Don't suppose that merely because you happen to be in the royal palace you will escape any more than the other Jews. ¹⁴ For if you fail to speak up now, relief and deliverance will come to the Jews from a different direction; but you and your father's family will perish. Who knows whether you didn't come into your royal position precisely for such a time as this."

¹⁵ Ester had them return this answer to Mordekhai: ¹⁶ "Go, assemble all the Jews to be found in Shushan, and have them fast for me, neither eating nor drinking for three days, night and day; also I and the girls attending me will fast the same way. Then I will go in to the king, which is against the law; and if I perish, I perish." ¹⁷ Then Mordekhai went his way and did everything Ester had ordered him to do.

When the Jews heard the news they cried out. Mordekhai tore his clothes, put on sackcloth and ashes publicly wailed loudly and bitterly. Ester sent one of the king's servants with clothes for him to put on instead of the sackcloth. But he refused to put them on. He told Ester about the new law, telling her to go into the king's presence to beg for mercy and plead to save her people, the Jews.

Ester told Mordekhai that anyone who approaches the king's inner courtyard, without being summoned by the king, is put to death – unless the king extends his golden scepter.

But Mordekhai said, *Just because you are in the royal palace doesn't mean you will escape any more than the other Jews. For if you fail to speak up now, deliverance will come to the Jews from a different direction; but you and your father's family will perish. Who knows whether you didn't come into your royal position precisely for such a time as this.*

Ester sent a reply to Mordekhai: *Gather all the Jews in Susa to pray and fast for me. Don't eat for three days. I will pray and fast with you. Then I will go to the king even though he has not summoned me. If I die, I die.*

5

¹ On the third day, Ester put on her royal robes and stood in the inner courtyard of the king's palace, opposite the king's hall. The king was sitting on his royal throne in the king's hall, across from the entrance to the hall. ² When the king saw Ester the queen standing in the courtyard, she won his favor; so the king extended the gold scepter in his hand toward Ester. Ester approached and touched the tip of the scepter. ³ "What is it you want, Queen Ester?" the king asked her. "Whatever your request, up to half the kingdom, it will be given to you." ⁴ "If it is all right with the king," answered Ester, "let the king and Haman come today to the banquet I have prepared for him." ⁵ The king said, "Bring Haman quickly, so that what Ester has asked for can be done." ⁽⁶⁾ So the king and Haman came to the banquet Ester had prepared.

⁶⁽⁷⁾ At the banquet of wine the king again said to Ester, "Whatever your request, you will be granted it; whatever you want, up to half the kingdom, it will be done." ⁷⁽⁸⁾ Then Ester answered, "My request, what I want, is this: ⁸ if I have won the king's favor, if it pleases the king to grant my request and do what I want, let the king and Haman come to the banquet which I will prepare for them; and tomorrow I will do as the king has said."

On the third day Ester put on her royal robes and stood in the inner court of the palace in front of the king's hall. When the king saw her, he was pleased and held out his golden scepter to her. *What is your request?* he asked. *Even if you ask for up to half the kingdom I will give it to you.*

I would like to invite the king and Haman to a special banquet I have prepared, Ester replied.

So the king and Haman went to the banquet. Again, he asked, *What is your request?*

Ester replied, *I would like to invite the king and Haman to another banquet tomorrow. Then I will answer the king's question.*

⁹ That day Haman went out happy and in good spirits. But when Haman saw Mordekhai at the King's Gate, that he neither rose nor moved for him, Haman was infuriated with Mordekhai. ¹⁰ Nevertheless, Haman restrained himself and went home, where he summoned and brought his friends and Zeresh his wife. ¹¹ Haman boasted to them about his vast wealth, his many sons, and everything connected with how the king had promoted him and given him precedence over the other officials and servants of the king. ¹² "Indeed," Haman added, "Ester the queen let nobody into the banquet with the king that she had prepared except myself; and tomorrow, too, I am invited by her, together with the king. ¹³ Yet none of this does me any good at all, as long as I keep seeing Mordekhai the Jew remaining seated at the King's Gate." ¹⁴ At this Zeresh his wife and all his friends said to him, "Have a gallows seventy-five feet high constructed, and in the morning speak to the king about having Mordekhai hanged on it. Then go in, and enjoy yourself with the king at the banquet." Haman liked the idea, so he had a gallows made.

Haman left the palace in a good mood but when he saw that Mordekhai had still not bowed or shown him respect, he was full of rage. Haman went to his friends and Zeresh his wife and boasted to them about his great wealth, his many sons and the ways the king had honored him. *I have been invited to a banquet by the king and queen tomorrow. But I cannot be happy while Mordekhai the Jew is sitting at the king's gate.*

His wife and friends had an idea. Ask the king to let you have Mordekhai killed. So he had a 75' gallows built from which to hang Mordekhai.

6

¹ That night, the king couldn't sleep; so he ordered the records of the daily journal brought, and they were read to the king. ² It was found written that Mordekhai had told about Bigtana and Teresh, two of the king's officers from the group in charge of the private entryways, who had conspired to assassinate King Achashverosh. ³ The king asked, "What honor or distinction was conferred on Mordekhai for this?" The king's servants answered, "Nothing was done for him." ⁴ The king then asked, "Who's that in the courtyard?" For Haman had come into the outer courtyard of the king's palace to speak to the king about hanging Mordekhai on the gallows he had prepared for him. ⁵ The king's servants told him, "It's Haman standing there in the courtyard." The king said, "Have him come in." ⁶ So Haman came in. The king said to him, "What should be done for a man that the king wants to honor?" Haman thought to himself, "Whom would the king want to honor more than me?" ⁷ So Haman answered the king, "For a man the king wants to honor, ⁸ have royal robes brought which the king himself wears and the horse the king himself rides, with a royal crown on its head. ⁹ The robes and the horse should be handed over to one of the king's most respected officials, and they should put the robes on the man the king wants to honor and lead him on horseback through the streets of the city, proclaiming ahead of him, 'This is what is done for a man whom the king wants to honor.'" ¹⁰ The king said to Haman, "Hurry, and take the robes and the horse, as you said, and do this for Mordekhai the Jew, who sits at the King's Gate. Don't leave out anything you mentioned."

¹¹ So Haman took the robes and the horse, dressed Mordekhai and led him riding through the streets of the city, as he proclaimed ahead of him, "This is what is done for a man whom the king wants to honor." ¹² Then Mordekhai returned to the King's Gate; but Haman rushed home with his head covered in mourning.

¹³ After Haman had told Zeresh his wife and all his friends everything that had happened to him, his advisers and his wife Zeresh said to him, "If Mordekhai, before whom you have begun to fall, is a Jew, you will not get the better of him; on the contrary, your downfall before him is certain."

¹⁴ While they were still talking with him, the king's officials came, hurrying to bring Haman to the banquet Ester had prepared.

That night the king couldn't sleep so he ordered the book that recorded details about his reign to be brought in and read to him. He heard the story of how Mordekhai had exposed the plot to kill him. He also discovered that nothing had been done to honor Mordekhai. Just then Haman came to ask the king to execute Mordekhai, but instead the king asked Haman what he thought should be done for a man the king wants to honor?

Haman thought the king was referring to himself so he answered, *Put a royal robe on the man and have him ride the king's horse led by a noble prince through the city, proclaiming, 'This is what is done for the man the king delights to honor!'*

Then the king told him to do this for Mordekhai. Haman felt humiliated. He went home and complained to his wife and friends, who told him that since Mordekhai was a Jew, he would not win against him.

7

¹ So the king and Haman went to Queen Ester's banquet; ² and the king again said to Ester at the wine banquet, "Whatever your request, Queen Ester, you will be granted it; whatever you want, up to half the kingdom, it will be done." ³ Ester the queen answered, "If I have won your favor, king, and if it pleases the king, then what I ask be given me is my own life and the lives of my people. ⁴ For we have been sold, I and my people, to be destroyed, killed, exterminated. If we had only been sold as men- and women-slaves, I would have remained quiet; since then [our] trouble would not have been worth the damage it would have caused the king [to alter the situation]." ⁵ King Achashverosh asked Ester the queen, "Who is he? Where is the man who dared to do such a thing?" ⁶ Ester said, "A ruthless enemy — it's this wicked Haman!" Haman stood aghast, terrified before the king and queen. ⁷ In a rage, the king got up from the wine banquet and went out to the palace garden. But Haman remained, pleading with Ester the queen to spare his life; for he could see that the king had decided to do him in. ⁸ Haman had just fallen on the couch where Ester was, when the king returned from the palace garden to the wine banquet. He shouted, "Is he even going to rape the queen here in the palace, before my very eyes?" The moment these words left the king's mouth, they covered Haman's face. ⁹ Harvonah, one of the king's attendants, said, "Look! The gallows seventy-five feet high that Haman made for Mordekhai, who spoke only good for the king, is standing at Haman's house." The king said, "Hang him on it." ¹⁰ So they hanged Haman on the gallows he had prepared for Mordekhai. Then the king's anger subsided.

8

¹ That same day King Achashverosh gave the house of Haman, the enemy of the Jews, to Ester the queen. Also Mordekhai appeared before the king, for Ester had revealed his relationship to her. ² The king removed his signet ring, which he had taken back from Haman, and gave it to Mordekhai. Then Ester put Mordekhai in charge of Haman's house.

Haman was then summoned to attend the banquet Queen Ester had prepared for him and the king. As they were drinking wine, the king asked, *What is your request? Even if it is half of my kingdom it will be granted.*

Ester replied, *My request is that you save my life and the lives of my people. We are to be destroyed.*

The king demanded to know, *Who has dared to threaten your life?*

An enemy, replied Ester, *this vile Haman.*

Haman looked terrified. The king got up in a rage and went outside. When he returned, it appeared that Haman had attacked Queen Ester. The king was angry, so one of his loyal assistants reminded him of the 75' gallows Haman had built, from which to hang Mordekhi.

The king said, *Hang him on it!* Then the king's fury subsided.

Ester then told the king she was related to Mordekha, so the king gave Mordekhai Haman's signet ring and Ester appointed him to look after Haman's riches and possessions.

³ Again Ester spoke to the king; she fell at his feet and begged him with tears to put an end to the mischief Haman the Agagi had caused by the scheme he had worked out against the Jews. ⁴ The king extended the gold scepter toward Ester. So Ester got up and stood in front of the king. ⁵ She said, "If it pleases the king, if I have won his favor, if the matter seem right to the king and if I have his approval, then let an order be written rescinding the letters devised by Haman the son of Hamdata the Agagi, which he wrote to destroy the Jews in all the royal provinces. ⁶ For how can I bear to see the disaster that will overcome my people? How can I endure seeing the extermination of my kinsmen?" ⁷ King Achashverosh said to Ester the queen and Mordekhai the Jew, "Listen! I gave Ester the house of Haman, and they hanged him on the gallows, because he threatened the lives of the Jews. ⁸ You should issue a decree in the king's name for whatever you want concerning the Jews, and seal it with the king's signet ring; because a decree written in the king's name and sealed with the king's ring can't be rescinded by anyone."

Then Ester fell at the king's feet weeping and begging him to put a stop to the evil plan to kill the Jews. *If it pleases the king, let an order be written overruling Haman's plan.*

The king said that no document written in his name could be changed; however another decree in his name and sealed with his signet ring could be written.

⁹ The king's secretaries were summoned at that time, on the twenty-third day of the third month, the month of Sivan; and a decree was written according to everything Mordekhai ordered concerning the Jews, to the army commanders, governors and officials of the provinces from India to Ethiopia, 127 provinces, to each province in its script and to each people in their language, also to the Jews in their script and language. ¹⁰ They wrote in the name of King Achashverosh and sealed it with the king's signet ring; they sent the letters by couriers on horseback riding fast horses used in the king's service and bred from the royal stock. ¹¹ The letters said that the king had granted the Jews in every city the right "to assemble and defend their lives by destroying, killing and exterminating any forces of any people or province that would attack them, their little ones or their women or would try to seize their goods as plunder ¹² on the designated day in any of the provinces of King Achashverosh, namely, the thirteenth day of the twelfth month, the month of Adar." ¹³ A copy of the edict was to be issued as a decree in every province and proclaimed to all the peoples, and the Jews were to be ready on that day to take vengeance against their enemies. ¹⁴ Couriers riding fast horses used in the king's service left quickly, pressed by the king's order; and the decree was issued in Shushan the capital.

¹⁵ Meanwhile, Mordekhai left the king's presence arrayed in royal blue and white, wearing a large gold crown and a robe of fine linen and purple; and the city of Shushan shouted for joy. ¹⁶ For the Jews, all was light, gladness, joy and honor. ¹⁷ In every province and city where the king's order and decree arrived, the Jews had gladness and joy, a feast and a holiday. Many from the peoples of the land became Jews, because fear of the Jews had overcome them.

So a new law was written to override the first decree, giving the Jews the right to gather and defend themselves if anyone attacked them. Copies of the new law were sent throughout the 127 provinces of the empire. Everyone knew the Jews would be ready and waiting if anyone attacked them on the 13th day of the 12th month (Adar). The Jews celebrated the news and their enemies became afraid of them.

9 ¹ The time approached for the king's order and decree to be carried out, the day when the enemies of the Jews hoped to overpower them. But, as it turned out, the opposite took place — the Jews overpowered those who hated them. Thus, on the thirteenth day of the twelfth month, the month of Adar, ² the Jews assembled in their cities throughout all the provinces of King Achashverosh to attack anyone who tried to do them harm; and no one was able to withstand them; because all the peoples were afraid of them. ³ All the officials of the provinces, the army commanders, the governors and those occupied with the king's affairs helped the Jews; because they were afraid of Mordekhai. ⁴ For Mordekhai had become a powerful person in the king's palace, and his fame had spread through all the provinces; Mordekhai continued to grow increasingly powerful.

⁵ The Jews put all their enemies to the sword; there was great slaughter and destruction, as they did whatever they wanted to those who hated them; ⁶ in Shushan the capital, the Jews slaughtered 500 men. ⁷⁻¹⁰ They put to death the ten sons of Haman the son of Hamdata, the enemy of the Jews — Parshandata, Dalfon, Aspata, Porata, Adalya, Aridata, Parmashta, Arisai, Aridai and Vaizata. But they did not touch the spoil.

¹¹ The same day, after the king had been told the number of those killed in Shushan the capital, ¹² he said to Ester the queen, "If the Jews have slaughtered 500 men in Shushan the capital and the ten sons of Haman, what have they done in the rest of the royal provinces! Now, whatever your request, you will be granted it; whatever more you want, it will be done." ¹³ Ester replied, "If it pleases the king, let the Jews in Shushan act again tomorrow in accordance with today's decree; also have Haman's ten sons hanged on the gallows." ¹⁴ The king ordered these things done — a decree was issued in Shushan, and they hanged Haman's ten sons. ¹⁵ So the Jews in Shushan assembled also on the fourteenth day of the month of Adar and killed 300 men in Shushan, but they did not touch the spoil.

¹⁶ The other Jews, those in the royal provinces, had assembled, defended their lives and won rest from their enemies, killing 75,000 of those who hated them, but without touching the spoil, ¹⁷ on the thirteenth day of the month Adar. So on the fourteenth day of Adar they rested and made it a holiday for celebrating and rejoicing. ¹⁸ However, the Jews of Shushan assembled on both the thirteenth and fourteenth days of Adar, so it was on the fifteenth that they rested and made it a holiday for celebrating and rejoicing. ¹⁹ This is why the Jews of the villages, those who live in unwalled towns, make the fourteenth day of the month of Adar a day for celebrating and rejoicing, a holiday and a time for sending each other portions [of food].

On the 13th day of the 12th month the enemies of the Jews tried to destroy them. The Jews gathered to defend themselves, helped by the governors and nobles of the provinces. Any group who hated the Jews and attacked them was defeated. But the Jews chose not to take any of their belongings even though the king said they could. Permission was given to the Jews to continue dealing with their enemies the next day also.

20 Mordekhai recorded these events and sent letters to all the Jews in all the provinces of King Achashverosh, both near and far, 21 instructing them to observe the fourteenth day of the month of Adar and the fifteenth day, every year, 22 [to commemorate] the days on which the Jews obtained rest from their enemies and the month which for them was turned from sorrow into gladness and from mourning into a holiday; they were to make them days of celebrating and rejoicing, sending portions [of food] to each other and giving gifts to the poor.

23 So the Jews took it upon themselves to continue what they had already begun to do, and as Mordekhai had written to them; 24 because Haman the son of Hamdata the Agagi, the enemy of the Jews, had plotted against the Jews to destroy them and had thrown *pur* (that is, "cast lots") to crush and destroy them; 25 but when Ester came before the king, he ordered by letters that [Haman's] wicked scheme, which he had plotted against the Jews, should recoil on his own head, and that he and his sons should be hanged on the gallows. 26 This is why these days have been called *Purim*, after the word *pur*. Thus, because of everything written in this letter, and what they had seen concerning this matter, and what had come upon them, 27 the Jews resolved and took upon themselves, their descendants and all who might join them that without fail they would observe these two days in accordance with what was written in [this letter] and at the appointed time, every year; 28 and that these days would be remembered and observed throughout every generation, every family, every province and every city; and that these days of *Purim* would never cease among the Jews or their memory be lost by their descendants.

29 Then Ester the queen, the daughter of Avichayil, and Mordekhai the Jew, gave full written authority to confirm a second letter about *Purim*. 30 He sent copies of it to all the Jews, to the 127 provinces of the kingdom of Achashverosh, ensuring their peace and security 31 and requiring the observance of these days of *Purim* at their designated times, as Mordekhai the Jew and Ester the queen had enjoined them, and as they had established for themselves and their descendants concerning the matters of fasting and lamenting. 32 At Ester's order these matters of *Purim* were confirmed and put in writing in the book.

10

1 King Achashverosh laid tribute on the land, the coasts and the islands. 2 All the acts of his power and might, along with a full account of the high honor to which the king advanced Mordekhai, are written in the Annals of the Kings of Media and Persia. 3 For Mordekhai the Jew was second only to King Achashverosh; he was a great man among the Jews, popular with all his many countrymen. He sought the good of his people and interceded for the welfare of all their descendants.

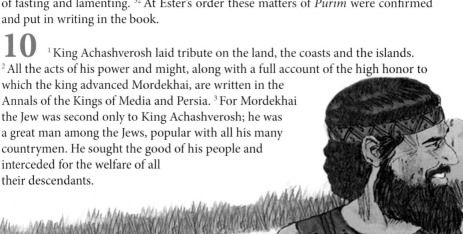

Mordekhai recorded all these events and sent letters to the Jews asking them to celebrate every year the Jews victory over their enemies on the 14th and 15th days of the 12th month. Haman had plotted and cast a lot, known as a *pur*, to destroy the Jews. So the celebration was called the Feast of *Purim*. It is a day of feasting and joy. People gave presents to each other. The Jews have kept this custom every year, throughout every generation, to this very day. Queen Ester ordered that all of this was put into a book.

Mordekhai the Jew became second only to King Achashverosh; he was a great man among the Jews, popular with all his many countrymen. He sought the good of his people and interceded for the welfare of all their descendants.

STUDY NOTES

1:1 These events took place in the time of Achashverosh. Achashverosh is also known as Ahasuerus and Xerxes, who ruled the Persian Empire approximately 486 to 469 B.C.E.

1:2 King Achashverosh sat on his royal throne in Shushan the capital. Shushan (Susa) was one of the Persian capital cities used during the winter months, and is found in southeast Iran today. Nechemyah (Nehemiah) served here in the king's court (Neh. 1:1), and Dani'el had a vision at this location (Dan. 8:2).

1:7 Drinks were served in gold goblets. Herodotus, the Greek historian, notes that Persians commonly drank liquor while they considered matters of state (see also 3:15), believing that its "spiritual effects" helped them to be in better touch with the "spiritual world."

2:1 When King Achashverosh's anger had subsided, he remembered Vashti. During the time period between 1:22 and 2:1, Achashverosh was involved in a disastrous invasion of Greece (481–480 B.C.E.) by both sea and land, with the Persians being expelled from Greece in 479. This means that after expelling Vashti, he chose Ester (Esther) as his new queen about six years later.

2:23 Both were hanged on a stake. The method of execution of being hanged on a stake was done, not by hanging the criminal by the neck, but by publically impaling him on a large stake or tree.

3:6 He decided to destroy all of Mordekhai's people, the Jews. Unfortunately, this pattern of a single man's hatred of Jews being made into public policy, which involves the destruction of whole Jewish populations, has reoccurred several times in Jewish history (e.g., Pharaoh, Haman, the Czars, and Hitler).

3:7 They began throwing pur. Haman's decision to set an execution date for Mordekhai's (Mordechai's) people was made by casting lots with a type of dice used to make various kinds of decisions. The *urim* and *thummim* mentioned in the book of Numbers (chs. 26–27) are a form of *pur* (see also Prov. 16:33; Acts 1:26). Thus the Hebrew name for the feast of Ester is *Purim*, the plural for *pur*.

3:10 The king took his signet ring from his hand and gave it to Haman. The king's signet ring represents the authority to carry out the king's edicts.

3:12 The king's secretaries were summoned on the thirteenth day of the first month. Ironically, the decree was sent out on the eve of *Pesach* (Passover).

4:4 When the girls and officials attending Ester came and informed her of this. In seeking Ester's intervention, Mordekhai is first required to inform her (cf. 3:8) of Haman's plan. Although queen over Shushan, Esther was secluded in the women's quarters and would have no access to outside political information apart from Hatakh's communiqué.

4:14 "Who knows whether you didn't come into your royal position precisely for such a time as this." Mordekhai appeals to Queen Ester that if she fails to act on behalf of her people, the massacre will also include her.

5:14 At this Zeresh his wife and all his friends said to him. These recommendations are much like the recommendations of Izevel (Jezebel) to Ach'av (Ahab) to kill a commoner "legally" so he could have what he wants (1 Kings 21:1–16). Haman was looking to make a large profit from confiscating Jewish possessions.

6:1 He ordered the records of the daily journals brought. According to Rashi, this was customary for the kings.

7:7–8 "Is he even going to rape the queen?" No one but the king would dare to be alone with the king's wife or a member of his harem. Haman should have left along with the king.

8:2 Then Ester put Mordekhai in charge of Haman's house. In Persia, as in many other ancient kingdoms, the estate of a traitor reverts to the crown. The two parts of Haman's "kingdom"—wealth and lands, along with the right to serve the king directly—revert to Ester and Mordekhai.

8:15 Mordekhai left the king's presence arrayed in royal blue and white. Mordekhai's robe is reminiscent of two other Jews who succeeded in the royal houses of other kingdoms, Yosef (Joseph) and Dani'el.

9:1–5 The Jews overpowered those who hated them. Since Persia's Jewish population was now allowed to defend itself by any means necessary, if anyone came against them on the "fateful day," they were now in charge, not Haman, and were allowed to fight to survive.

9:10 They put to death the ten sons of Haman....But they did not touch the spoil. Since Mordekhai was from the tribe of Binyamin (Benjamin), the text is careful to say that he did not repeat the mistakes of Sha'ul (Saul), the Benjamite king, who kept the spoils of the 'Amaleki (Amalekites). Agag is the 'Amaleki king directly responsible for Sha'ul's downfall (see 1 Sam. 14–15). In 3:1, Haman is called an Agagi (Agagite). In this way, the ancient enmity between Isra'el and 'Amalek is reflected in the relationship between Mordekhai and Haman.

9:27 They would observe these two days in accordance with what was written. *Purim* is to be celebrated for all time, the first holiday outside of the *Torah* to be designated as such. Other holidays subsequently established are *Hanukkah* and *Tisha B'Av* (the "Ninth of Av," a day of mourning).